# THE SPIRIT OF HÚNIR AWAKENS

## QUESTIONS & ANSWERS

By Frank A. Rúnaldrar

## HIGH GALDR SERIES
Book One: The Breath of Oðin Awakens (2$^{nd}$ Ed)
Book Two: The Spirit of Húnir Awakens (Part 1)
Book Three: The Spirit of Húnir Awakens (Part 2)

## QUESTIONS & ANSWERS SERIES
The Breath of Oðin Awakens - Questions & Answers
The Spirit of Hunir Awakens - Questions & Answers

# THE SPIRIT OF HÚNIR AWAKENS

## Questions
## &
## Answers

*by*
Frank A. Rúnaldrar

Part of the High Galdr Series
www.highgaldr.com

Published in 2018 by:
Bastian & West
www.bastianandwest.com

Copyright © 2018 Frank A. Rúnaldrar

The moral right of the author has been asserted.

All rights reserved. No part of this publication may be reproduced or transmitted in any form or by any means, electronic or mechanical, including photocopying, recording, or by any information storage and retrieval system, without permission in writing from the copyright holder. Reviewers may quote brief passages.

**Part of High Galdr Series - Questions & Answers**
www.highgaldr.com/qa

ISBN: 978-0-9955343-5-3

A CIP catalogue record for this book is available from the British Library.

Cover based on design by: Judge a Cover Designs

Book typeset in Niva Light by PeGGO Fonts, Norse font by Joël Carrouché and runic elements in Felt-Tip Futhark by Thomas Kaeding

**Copyright Notice:** All rights, title and interests in the copyrights to all materials (including but not limited to any proprietary knowledge, data, information, manuals, illustrations, diagrams, flowcharts, marks or other information therein contained or thereby disclosed and representing the author's original works), are hereby reserved and to be considered the exclusive property of and belong exclusively to the author. The purchase of this book by any person(s), and its usage by any other party, shall not be construed as granting or conferring any rights by license or otherwise to the purchasing party or any other party who may come in possession of the book and/or its materials. No part of this publication or its materials may be reproduced, distributed, disseminated, or transmitted in any form or by any means and for any purpose, including but not limited to photocopying, recording, or other electronic or mechanical methods, without the prior written permission and consent of the author, except in the case of brief quotations embodied in critical reviews and certain other non-commercial used permitted by copyright law. In the event any reader or third party submits to the author or the publisher, either jointly or severally, any questions, then any questions based on, derived from or incorporating any of the author's materials in this publication, together with any answers provided by the author, if any, shall be deemed to be works derived from the author's copyrighted materials and accordingly such reader or third party in submitting its questions irrevocably agrees to the exclusive and royalty free world wide transfer and assignment (free of costs) of all or any rights, title or benefit in such questions to the owner for its discretionary use in any format and by any medium.

**Usage Disclaimer:** It is expressly agreed and acknowledged by all and any reader(s) and any parties that come into possession of the materials that all materials, information, techniques, methods, processes or statements made in this publication, and all and any associated materials as may be derived therefrom and distributed from time to time in any written or tangible forms and in any media (including electronic media), as the case may be, by the author or its publisher(s), are for to be used strictly for educational purposes only (the "Permitted Purpose") and not for any other personal or commercial purpose. All materials reflect the author's personal views and opinions, and no method or process or statement or anything else said in the materials is to be treated as having any scientific value, validity or status. Under no circumstances whatsoever or howsoever are any materials in this book, in whole or in part, intended to operate as scientifically proven methods, processes or statements, or intended to offer any medical or other advise, or be used in substitute for medical advise of and/or treatment by physicians for any matters. Neither the author nor its publisher(s) make any statement, representation, guarantee or undertaking howsoever or whatsoever as to the usefulness of any materials. The use of the materials for any other purpose, including any personal or commercial purposes other than for educational purposes, contrary to the Permitted Purpose, is not promoted and strictly prohibited. The author and its publisher(s) accept no risk, responsibility or liability for any unsanctioned use, which shall be at the user's sole risk, and shall, together and severally (the "Released and Indemnified Parties"), be held harmless and indemnified by any users engaging in any unsanctioned use contrary to this disclaimer from all and any claims, rights, liabilities, demands, obligations, conditions, promises, acts, costs, expenses, accountings, damages or actions of whatsoever kind or nature, whether in law or otherwise, whether known or unknown, which they made have or may thereafter have against the Released and Indemnified Parties for or by any reason of any occurrence, matter or thing which arise or are claimed to have arisen out of or in connection with any such unsanctioned use of the materials.

I would like to dedicate this book to all those who have read the Spirit of Húnir Awakens

# Table of Content

## Trance, Awareness & Perception Questions
- Trouble Shifting into Rune Shapes ..........................1
- Dropping In and Out of Trance .................................3
- Mental Seeing ..................................................................5
- Silencing The Mind, Is There Any Point? ................7
- Carrying Over Memories (From Trance States) .....15
- Mental Perceptions - Real or Illusory ....................17

## Projection Questions
- Óðr Projection, Hurg or Minni Raven Flight? ...............23
- Mental / Spirit or Astral Projection? ..........................29
- Difficulties Projecting .............................................33
- Failing To Fully Project with Hugr ..........................35
- Loosing the Hugr or The Minni? ..............................37

## Healing The Mind - Improving Life
- Dealing with Obsessions and Addictions ...............41
- Using 'Like Attracts Like' to Improve Life .............45

## Deep Theory
- Energy, Runes, 'Magic' are They Real? ..................51
- Spirit Vibrational Rates and Time ............................57
- Why Do Spirits Seek Love? .....................................61
- Masculine vs Feminine Biological Polarities .........65
- Rune Mystics and Religious Practices ....................69

## Appendix
- References & footnotes .............................................75

## Preface

I would like to start by thanking all those of you with whom I have had the pleasure to enter into deep conversations on *The Spirit of Húnir Awaken* [1,5] topics. It is always a delight to see how this work can lead to such depth of thinking.

In this Q&A are some in-depth answers to the most common questions received. Additionally, I have added a couple of 'deep theory' short-essays written in order to elucidate some of the applications and provide additional theoretical insights. I do hope these prove to be of interest and provide you with further insights!

# TRANCE, AWARENESS & PERCEPTION

# Trouble Shifting into Rune Shapes

*Q: I am having trouble with shifting into the shapes of the runes.*

I have always found this to be one of the most difficult practices. We are so used to seeing ourselves in our physical shapes that these shapes become ingrained in our perceptions and define what and who we are.

In actual fact our spirit does not even pervade our physical bodies (Lik) until we learn how to make it do so. It seems odd therefore that our physical shapes seem so inescapable.

What the practice of 'Óðr Shaping into Runes – Becoming The Rune Flow'[1] is designed to do is twofold. First it is used to loosen the bonds our physical form has on our perceptions. Second, the practice of shaping into a rune, followed by another, then another, into what is nothing more than a simple geometric shape, where no cognition is possible, acts as a type of reset mechanisms on many levels of the Self. As a rune you do not do anything, you do not think, you take no action, you just ARE and learn to just BE.

As you work on your development, the key is to understand that your shifting into the rune does not have to be "total". It takes many years of constant practice to achieve a complete shift. What you want to achieve is simply a shifting into the rune and identifying yourself with the rune for a brief period of time. To begin with aim for 5-10 seconds. A couple of seconds is all you need, PROVIDING you feel and perceive yourself as the rune during that time! When you have mastered that, try a few minutes and see what that gives.

## Dropping In and Out of Trance

Q: 'I switch to being conscious in the Óðr, can maintain it for a day or so then forget about it and loose my focus'

This is perfectly normal. Do to worry about it or beat yourself up over loosing focus occasionally. As we are expanding awareness (which is what you are doing by using the 'Becoming Conscious of the Óðr (Spirit)'[2]) you will shift into enhanced awareness and drop out of it, often on a loop. It is a new state which you will need to learn and adapt to.

With awareness, especially conscious awareness, BOTH the mind and the body need to learn to function at a new 'enhanced' level. You may find that you will need more energy to maintain perceptual focus at this heightened level which in turn explains why it is perfectly normal that you drop out when your energy levels fizzle out. As with anything, perseverance is key.

When you drop out of enhanced awareness simply acknowledge it and slip back into it. Your focus and attention should be geared towards re-establishing the Óðr shift as soon as you notice you have slipped out of it. Eventually, over time, you will find it easier and easier to maintain these enhanced states of awareness. By the same token, the dropping out will die down and become less frequent.

Bear in mind that it will be more difficult to master the practice where you are impacting biological awareness, as opposed to just working on the mental / spiritual levels of your Self. Persistence, persistence, persistence. Pick yourself up each time you fall out of sync and get back into the flow. Teaching your brain and your spirit how to shift from one state of awareness to another will help you with more advanced forms of awareness manipulation.

At this point you are just working on shifting from the automatically driven daily awareness to one of multiple layers of reality within your Self. Later on you will be working on shifting from what is now an 'enhanced' state to even more profound states of awareness and perception. Leaning how to make these shifts occur will make it easier later to achieve the far more complex expansions of conscious awareness.

# Mental Seeing

Q: *When images pop into my mind am I seeing them? is this clairvoyance?*

We tend to forget that since we are not only physical beings, our senses function on multiple levels of reality, and we do have the inherent ability to perceive the non-physical. Some confusion comes about the fact that typically we only FOCUS on using our sensory apparatus to perceive the physical, and outwardly apparent to everyone.

What is happening here when images pop in your mind is that your focus is shifting. No doubt, through practice, your focus is shifting into the other parts of reality and hence your perceptions are picking up information via the senses from other sources. The brain ultimately interprets the information and converts it into terms that are familiar to it, i.e. imagery, sound, sensation and so forth.

What you are experiencing is perception at a direct mental level. In other words, images 'popping' directly into your mind. Some see them as memories, others perceive them as sceneries but without the actual physical images which generate those in the first place. The brain interprets what your senses have picked up directly from the source of energy you have tapped into. This is a common occurrence in trance states or when you alter your level of awareness.

Are these perceptions clairvoyance? Traditionally speaking, yes. Remember clairvoyance means clear-seeing. When seeing with the mental eye, you have the most accurate clairvoyance. There is no interpretation, there is no conversion, only seeing as is for what it is. From the energetic level it is less 'clear', and from the physical even less so (because these levels of perception are subject to perceptual interpretation).

Label it what you will, sight is sight, no matter what level of reality we choose to use it on.

# SILENCING THE MIND
## IS THERE ANY POINT?

*Q: Silencing the Mind – Is there Any Point? – Will I Stop Thinking? Will I Stop Being?*

Silencing the mind is essential if you want to make progress in developing your perception.

The concept of a silent mind can be quite daunting. Some people fear they will 'stop' thinking. Others that they will no longer have access to their memories, ideas or the ability to logically work things out. Religion and other theological schools of thought have done their best to promote the idea that an 'empty' mind allows other 'things' to enter and fill the void, such that the mind to be hijacked.

It is important to understand that when silencing your mind you are not emptying it or losing any ability (or memory for that fact). What you are seeking to achieve by practicing clearing your mind is to slow down the onslaught of mental chatter and hopefully stop it. This will allow you to take control of the flow of thoughts coming into your mind from the mental levels of reality.

What we term 'minds' are in effect complex processing mechanisms of the Spirit (Óðr). It is the Spirit (Óðr) which receives mental inputs and process them into more developed outputs. These inputs are your thoughts. As we process them, adding to them, thinking of them, analysing them and so forth, you add more 'weight' or complexity to those thoughts and turn them into 'thought streams'. This process imbues those thoughts with energy, and hence gravity, which in turn allows them to manifest.

Silencing the mind allows you to call a break in this constant onslaught of inputs into your mind. By calling a temporary break, not only do you gain the ability to save mental energy but to have a 'helicopter' view of what is going throughout the mind rather than being overflowed with constant streams of thought.

It is always easier to be objective when you are looking into a situation rather than being part of it. When you are in the flow, you are effected by it, you harmonise with it and it carries us along. This is true for life, relationships, personal and professional situations, and so forth. Taking a step back allows for perspective on situations (flows) you find yourself in, and with perspective the opportunity to act on the situation from your own Will and Self rather than by default driven by the direction of the flow of things. This logic applies to all things including your thoughts.

Why would you want to do this with your own thinking, you may ask? The simple answer is that as long as you are in control of the current flow of your thoughts (which are not technically speaking all your own in the first place), you direct your mind and the totality of all its powers and abilities. Since the mind

(Hugr) is the active manifestation of the Spirit (Óðr), the mind (Hugr) is directing the Spirit (Óðr) too. Take a moment and think about this: we are all influenced by our environments on a constant basis. This includes our friends (including their thoughts and opinions, media and advertising we are exposed to on a constant basis, politics, arguments advanced in favour of one cause or another. The list goes on. All these things direct our minds and Spirits (Óðr) whether we want them to or not. Additionally, we will see in *The Blood of Lóðurr Awakens*[3] how our biology does exactly the same thing albeit using a different mechanism. Our thoughts, our preferences, our behavioural patters, likes and dislikes are constantly impacted by the external as well as the internal. Talking of biology, ever thought about the fact that our bodies are chemical organisms? Ever wondered how chemistry effects the body which then effects the mind and its thought streams? Yes, our environment dictates our thinking and not just socially. By the same token, genetics, chemistry, and viral influence and so forth constantly affect thinking. Such factors or influencers are seldom spoken off, no doubt since we are typically unaware of them because they are subtle and indirect. There is no hiding from the fact that all these factors or influencers which impact the body, in turn impact the mind. We will look at this in a lot more at a later point in time.

There is yet another category of influencing sources: that is, the spiritual and / or archetypal. Our core Self needs experiences to grow and develop. Our Fylgja needs them, our ancestry needs them. All those spirits we have in our lives, whether perceived or not, have an influencing impact on our minds, our thinking and our own spirit. They inspire thoughts, courses of actions and in somecases even obsessions. Some may call this 'guidance' from our 'Higher Self'. Others will put their own label on it, typically attributing positive impulses to the work of 'God', 'Gods', guardians, ancestors or something else perceived to be innately good or nourishing to the Self. Conversely, negative inspiration will be attributed to immediately opposing forces, the 'devil', demons, villainous beings, a nemesis or ancestral enemy, or something else perceived to be innately evil or destructive to the Self. It matters not whether this is positive or negative, whether they come from the Self or an external source. What matters is that all these 'factors' or 'forces' influence our thought patterns and thought streams, and by so doing shape or form expressions of the Spirit (Óðr), what it will experience and the direction in which it will be journey. The most powerful of these influences is: Ørlǫg (personal fate). Ørlǫg directs us in our path through life. Not all influences are negative or 'bad'. Influences will however manipulate and reshape our awareness and wills. This is why, with the arrival of the Norns in Norse mythology, it is said that the golden age of the Gods ended as these fate weaving Giantesses imposed the rigid flow of fate on Creation and the Gods themselves.

 With all these influences grounding us in our daily lives, there is no 'room' for spiritual or energetic realities. This is one of the primary reasons why most people are unable to perceive those parts of reality.

 By silencing the mind, you temporarily push the breaks on truck-tones of mental influences, take a deep breath and gain the ability to find a foothold, refocus the Self, regain control of your Spirit (Óðr).

 You might wonder what happens when you silence the mind and apply these metaphoric breaks to the constant chit chatter of your mind? Well, you gain stillness. It is very much like being in the eye of a cosmic storm of thinking. This stillness allows for perceptions to reset to their natural order; a setting not directed by thinking, words or needs. Think about it as the removal of all filters imposed on your perceptions. when the filter is removed, you stand still. As you do, your actual Self surfaces from the daily cacophony imposed on it by the mind when confounded by all the influencers around it.

These stirrings of the Self will initially be extremely short, a moment or two at most. With practice, they will grow in time to a few second until eventually, as you gain the ability to sit in silence and stillness, they grow into minutes on end. Your energetic Self will in the process stir and surface, your awareness become more focused and perception sharpened. Eventually, after long practice, you will not only become able to consciously direct your will and mind at a single specific thought of your own picking but also maintain it without interruption or interference. The stronger your focus, the more powerful your will. This is an excellent gauge of actual strength of will and power. Those who are carried in the wind of thoughts are powerless. Those who can stand firm in the eye of the storm are manifesting the actual power of Will. Simple, fundamental fact.

As you keep on doing this your perceptions shift to those of your actual Self and Spirit. You start to perceive energy first, then physicality of reality second, rather than just perceiving its physicality and getting intuitive hints (typically dismissed) at the energetic. In addition to this, as your mind regains its natural mode of function, it also regains all skills that are inherently part of that natural functioning. Shifting through levels of perception, instant boundless knowing and much more, simply open up. This type of knowing is what we are all born with, and taught to eliminate during childhood schooling when institutionalisation and social integration training starts. Remember when you were at school how you were forced to always show your workings (especially in sciences, maths, computing and so forth?) why? It is not to prove that you had the correct answer that is evident. It was to built a filter on direct knowing. By being forced to work things out in a specific prescribed fashion you were teaching your biology and mind rigid patterns which it needed to comply with. Over time, the mind fits its perceptions into those patterns, and each time it would try to expand perceptive / mental abilities it would be bound by those very patterns and limitations accordingly defined. Once the mind gets accustomed to one set of patterns, it breeds the fear of the unknown (lack of pattern based thinking) which it seeks to avoid at all costs. Effectively the mind becomes conditioned for life to established social standards of thinking, and any thinking outside of those parameters considered 'foreign', a fear or threat.

When silencing our minds, we do not remove those patterns, we simply turn them off. It takes a LOT of practice to completely remove them, if at all possible. By turning them off we suddenly take off the mental shackles imposed upon our Spirits (Óðr) and allow them to reset in their infinite natures. Even if done for only a few moments at a time, rewards are great. The more often we enter stillness and silence the more accustomed we become to working outside of those imposed conditions and the broader and richer our experiences, knowledge, perceptions and Spirit (Óðr) become. We stop being mental and spiritual sheep. We Evolve.

This is just how important silencing of the mind actually is. It allows us to broaden our experiences. We are able to reach out for more, new and unfamiliar things, thoughts and energies. That in turn opens up new possibilities, new avenues, new opportunities.

That is one of the fundamental mysteries the rune ♦ Ár (Jera) speaks off: the stepping out of an existing cycle into a greater one, which in turn is then stepped out of into a yet higher one and so it continues, evolves. When we get to studying the actual runes and their energies we will see how these thought-streams can be used to flow with the runes in order to access their treasuries of knowledge, experiences and powers to further our own cycles of evolution

## - The Spirit of Húnir - Questions & Answers -

## Carrying Over Memories (From Trance States)

*Q: When in Trance I Perceive and Remember Things Perfectly but as Soon as I Get Out of Trance It all Becomes Blurred and is Quickly Forgotten. Why is That?*

This is an energy deficit issue. It takes a large amount of energy to carry over memories from higher states of awareness to lower states. Here, when we are discussing energy, it is not simply energy but rather a substance. It is the amount of power or punch your energy has. In Norse terms we would be referring to Megin (see *The Breath of Odin Awakens*[4]) rather than simple energy.

Memories are carried over by the Minni to the everyday or mundane consciousness. When experienced in the higher states of awareness however they are inscribed in either the Fylgja or the energy body (Hamr). When attempting to carry energetic substance over from one state to the other, you need to undergo a type of transcribing process from the one to the other and for that to occur there is a large energy requirement.

It is fascinating to note that you do not always NEED to carry memories over. Memories are always going to be available in those heightened states. They are not lost when you exit the heighted state. If not transported they are merely left behind. So all you need to do is to shift back into that elevated state of awareness where you had the experience in the first place to remember it in order to regain perfect clarity recall (or alternatively use the memory practices provided in *The Spirit of Húnir Awakens (Part 2)*[5]). It is actually more than a simple recall as we would typically understand it. It is more akin to a direct immediate reliving of those experiences rather than just remembering them as you would physically.

If you do want to or need to actually recall those memories whilst in everyday or mundane awareness, you will need to fuel your Minni with Megin before shifting into heightened awareness and transcribe the memories for you. More advanced work in this field teaches how to expand the memory systems with the assistance of our biological awareness (see *The Blood of Lóðurr Awakens*[3]) in order to bridge the two forms of awareness seamlessly.

# Mental Perceptions
## Real or Illusory?

*Q: How Do I Know if What I am Mentally Perceiving is Illusory or Real?*

    This is a difficult question one that can only be answered with experience. There are two types of 'real' when dealing with mental perceptions. The first is actual and the other is imagined. They are both 'real' to a certain extent. How 'real' you can consider what is imagined depends on the density that whatever you imagine has. In other words, you can imagine something until eventually it gains the respective energetic gravity required for it to become real. In most cases this take a lot of time and effort to achieve.

    The distinction is an easier one to make when you are trying to perceive something with any one of your mental senses. The first trick is to look at whatever you are observing closely and see whether it is generating energy or not. All things in creation which exist generate some form of energy, even objects in our daily lives pulse faint energy patterns. If whatever you observe is not, then it would not be considered real. The other trick is to simply imagine that whatever you are observing has changed drastically into something else. The rule of thumb is that if there is a transformative change, it is a product of your imagination. This is not fool-proof. There are always exceptions to the rule. I, myself, prefer and would recommend using the energy generating trick.

    This is one of the reasons why when you are working on developing your ability to mentally project (Óðr / Spirit Projection) you spend a minimum of about six months practicing looking at your own body and your immediate environment from within the Spirit (Óðr) BEFORE going wandering off. This helps not only solidify the Spirit (Óðr) but also solidify your perceptions by allowing you to verify them after each practice until what you perceive from within your Spirit (Óðr) matches perfectly what you see with your physical eyes. Those who project and then start wandering off without mastering this lose themselves in wonderful yet totally imagined 'realms'. The entire ability then becomes nothing more than self-deluding and non-gratifying day-dreaming.

    A better method is to shift your awareness into the object or subject being observed. If it has a centre point of gravity, it is real. If everything fades away, indicating that there is no point of centrality, then it is imagined. This is a tricky reference to use, and one which we will cover at a later point in time when learning about the Spark of the Self.

    The distinction between the imagined and real in terms of practices is easy to make once you have become accustomed to noticing the differences in between the two. When working with energy for instance, you start by imagining a new energy, after long practice it will start to manifest all of its characteristics spontaneously. Let us put this into context. When you start working with a rune, say, ᚠ Fé (Fehu), you would imagine its blazing red, hot expansive energy and imagine its name echoing within that energy. After a while, you will notice that just thinking of ᚠ Fé (Fehu)'s energy will spontaneously manifest vast expanses of this type of energy without having to even think about the heat, the sounds of rune name pronounced or its expansive power. They will all manifest automatically. This spontaneous manifestation of the runic energy's characteristics is what indicates that you are working with the real energy rather than its imagined counterpart. Another good indicator is where the spontaneous manifestation of characteristics is much much stronger than those you previously imagined. What you do here is use your imagination to trigger the 'like attracts like' on the mental level of reality. After a while the real ᚠ Fé (Fehu) energy responds to the 'likeness' you broadcasted out. In other words, the real ᚠ Fé (Fehu) energy overrides that which you formally imagined because when using real energies, they embed themselves in your consciousness and the real displaces what was once only imaginary. One always defaults to the real version.

It bears mentioning that with energies, the same reality checking as set out above applies. Remember, any real energy you work with will emanate energy! (Naturally!).

# PROJECTION

# Óðr Projection, Hugr or Minni Raven Flight?

*Q: What is the Difference Between Óðr Projection, Hugr Raven Flight and Mini Raven Flight?*

An excellent question. These all represent different parts of the Self AND different types of perceptive awareness. For this reason, when you project in one rather than the other the scope of what you can achieve and perceive is very different. We will look at each in turn.

Huge Raven Flight[7]: as we have discussed in *The Spirit of Húnir Awakens (Part 1)*, the Hugr is our mind, our logic, our thinking capability as well as our processing ability. It is the perfect vehicle for what we typically understand as our consciousness. Due to its similarity with 'standard' consciousness, all the perceptual and awareness skills we develop in our daily lives are fully functional during Hugr Projection. Our ability to consciously observe, think about, analyse and react according to our typical thinking modes of action are all available. It is actually the fundamental way of functioning within the Hugr. Seeing as it is also the active part of the Spirit (Óðr), our Will comes into play as well.

Minni Raven Flight[8]: this type of projection represents the complete opposite to the Hugr one. Here we do not have any thinking, deducting and analysing abilities available. When projecting using the Minni Raven you end up in a passive type of trance-like state where you simply observe and remember. It is almost entirely instinctive. The will or ability to direct consciously is practically completely absent during the Minni Raven Flight. One MAJOR advantage of using the Minni rather than the Hugr is that none of the constraints of the conscious are in play either. With the former you would only be able to go to realities you are consciously familiar with, know how to enter and handle, and so forth. Since the Minni is purely instinctive, you need no knowledge of where you are going, how to get there or anything else that may direct your 'flight' path. All you need is a desire to be there. This means that in most cases when you try to reach an energetic level of reality which is beyond your ability to deal with, you can reach it with far greater ease by using the Minni than the Hugr. Memories of those realities will get integrated via the ritual of the Sumbl or memory practices (see *The Spirit of Húnir Awakens (Part 2)*[5]) with your conscious perception. As you build up your catalogue of memories in this manner, your conscious awareness will start to conceive those other realities, recognise their energies, patterns and laws. Eventually this merging will enable you to directly interact with those realities so that you can simply switch to Hugr projection instead to consciously interact with them.

One thing to note which was not mentioned in *The Spirit of Húnir Awakens (Part 2)*[5] is that the Minni has a strong connection to our biological awareness (typically misinterpreted as the subconscious). In effect, this means that your learning path will take you in the opposite direction to what you would typically do. Most human learning is by logic and hence the Hugr. What is learn is then experientially transferred to the biological awareness (our body's intellect). With Minni projection, there is a deviation from this learning path. You will go from the physical / energetic upwards to the mental. The Minni writes the memories into the physical body (Lik) and energy systems and then these memories are eventually transmitted by experiential learning to the mind (Hugr) and Spirit (Óðr). This learning method is termed 'receptive learning'. When combined with the usual "mind-to-body" learning method (typically termed 'active learning'), it offers a highly significant enhancement of all levels of the Self and the key abilities such two way communications bring such as the ability to carry knowledge from higher states of awareness into physical logical awareness flawlessly and with little effort.

Spirit (Óðr) projection, is a completely different matter. Here you are separating the root manifestation of the Self on the spiritual level. It shares most of the characteristics of both the Hugr and the Minni, and additionally has a whole host of its own. The main difficulty with Spirit (Óðr) projection is that it is not naturally formed. It has no shape and as such is very difficult to start working with. This is the primary reason why we undertake the effort of shaping the projection as we learn to separate it. This very process can take months, in not years, of daily practice. Then, providing we have shaped it to a perfect replica of our physical form, we can start to will the consciousness to be hosted within it and use it as a vehicle.

You might wander why shape it exactly like the physical body (Lik)? The simple answer is that this is the shape we are familiar with AND the shape dictates the energy system (and vice versa). If there is a mismatch between the two, the flow of energy in between the Spirit (Óðr) and the energy system will be interrupted so that full consciousness cannot be maintained. Instead, you will be left with a semi-aware type of daydream or wishful thinking 'wonderful' trips which have absolutely no basis in actual reality. That is of course assumes that consciousness can be maintained with all the mismatching.

The problematic part with spirit (Óðr) projecting is that you need to have the mental side of the Self active together with the energetic and physical. When mastering this skill, you are not only hosting awareness but also consciousness (which is dependant on the biological awareness). Effectively, you are weaving spiritual awareness with the biological awareness into the Spirit (Óðr). Once this has been mastered, we learn to perceive from within it directly.

Our spirits are not all knowing or all powerful as most assume. Our spirits, for most, are infants learning to take their first steps. Once you learn to host your full conscious awareness in the spirit (Óðr), the next step is to learn to perceive from within it directly. It is all too familiar with perceiving with the help of the physical sensory apparatus, but now you are teaching it to perceive directly without recourse to the physical. When this has been mastered the next step is to learn to initiate action from within it. Even to transfer the impulse to move, turn, shift, without the physical body's support systems, is a process that needs to be learnt from afresh. At this point you are not only learning to move but also teaching your biological awareness how to operate without its underlying biology. Think of it as teaching each and every cell in your body, every organ, every nerve, every blood cell, every iota without you, how to project, be and operate in the spirit (Óðr). For this reason we start by learning how to move as if we were in a physical body (Lik) within the spirit (Óðr), even though there is no physical body there.

Finally, when all this has been perfectly mastered, you will learn to unleash intent within the Spirit (Óðr) without any support of the energetic or physical systems. Mastering this is what gives you the ability to shift into other realities or energetic states.

In addition to all of this, at each stage of learning we use the conscious mind to check and double check and triple check whether what we are experiencing matches Midgard reality. This verification process is meant to assure that the Spirit (Óðr) is taught to only perceive actual reality and able to cut through the illusory nonsense. It is only once absolute certainty of perception is gained that full use of the Spirit (Óðr) projection in non-physical realities can be achieved.

It is a long learning curve but worth every hard step taken along the journey. When full mastery is gained, and mastery of all the various energies obtained, there is no ceiling to what can be actually achieved.

We will look at Spirit (Óðr) and energy body (Hamr) projection in a lot more detail at a later point in time.

- The Spirit of Húnir - Questions & Answers -

#  Mental / Spirit or Astral Projection?

Q: *Is There a Distinction Between Mental Spirit Projection and Astral Projection?*

The answer to this question depends entirely on what you refer to as the 'astral'. It is a very ambiguous term with a definition which seems to be ever expanding. Some use astral projection to refer to mental projection (Óðr / Spirit projection). Others use it to describe day-dreaming. Others yet use it to describe lucid dreaming and a whole further host of different projections. For the purposes of these teachings, we will use the original meaning which is projection of the energy body (Hamr).

The distinction between both terms lies in the scope and perceptual ability whilst projecting. With spirit or mental projection, you can reach levels of reality which you cannot with energy body (Hamr) projection. The later simply cannot reach those levels of vibration. With energy body (Hamr) projection however, you can reach far superior energetic perceptions. Put otherwise, projection of the energy body (Hamr) results in far closer or 'real life' perceptions whereas mental / spirit projection provides far subtler or abstract perceptions at a higher level of reality.

Physiologically speaking, with energy body (Hamr) projection we carry our biological awareness fused with our spirits. This explains why users of this type of separation of the Self appear to be dead physically when in session. Their physical bodies (Lik) will breath only rarely, so rarely in fact that to any onlooker will have the impression they are not breathing at all. Their skin will turn a very pale colour and resemble the place blue colour of corpses. Their hearts will beat only very scarcely, on a very long pattern, seemingly not beating at all between every very long interval. This state of "suspended animation" of the physical body (Lik) is a result of real astral projection. This is also where all the warnings and dangers of becoming lost are highly relevant. Left unsecured, the physical body (Lik) is opened to attack and hijack from other beings who may desire to step into it and taking hold of it. These dangers do NOT apply with mental / spirit projection.

In terms of conscious awareness, astral projection puts you in a state of pure ecstasy, your consciousness goes into overdrive, pure energy perception ensues. The entire experience is an absolute thrill and you will be buzzing as if you have just stepped off a exhilarating rollercoaster ride. It is very much like turning into hyper-drive mode, both energetically and perceptually.

With mental or spirit projection, any onlooker will simply see you as being either in meditation or think you are sleeping. Only consciousness and awareness are separated from the physical body (Lik), rather than the entire energy system. Biological awareness remains firmly seated in your physical body (Lik) and hence all biological functions will appear to be perfectly normal and stable. You will have heighted perceptions and an overriding sense of freedom but it will fall short of the ecstasy of real astral projection. However, due to the lack of biological awareness, being projected you will enjoy far subtler forms of energy and far looser conformity to shape or form. Pure spirit projection has no form and that in itself can be a mesmerising experience.

# Difficulties Projecting

Q: *I practiced the mental Óðr projection and am having trouble separating and staying out...*

This comes with practice. At first you will part separate, staying aware and conscious of all your physical body (Lik) and your separated Spirit (Óðr). Then you will progress to being aware of only being in Spirit but for very brief periods of time. These can be so brief that they may last only a split second or two. Eventually as you persevere further, your awareness will be completely within the Spirit and you will become oblivious to the physical, first for several seconds, then for a minute, and eventually for several minutes and so forth. Practice on a daily basis is key. Readers that reported achieving full projection after practicing twice daily for 2 to 3 weeks are lucky. The average time frame, depending on frequency of practice over that period, is around 3 to 6 months.

The reason it takes time is firstly that, you are teaching your conscious awareness to function without relying on the physical body (Lik). Your conscious awareness has never had to do this before. Second, you are teaching your Spirit (Óðr) to not only maintain form but to replicate your physical shape to the smallest detail without being able to rely on it. Third, you are teaching your conscious awareness to not only maintain that form and move from within it, but also to actively perceive through it. When you have done all of that, fourth, you then need to teach your conscious awareness to distinguish between that which is real and that which is not. After all of that, fifth, additionally you will need to teach your brain (and conversely your physiology) how to assimilate all of the experiences, memories and perceptions back into normal consciousness so that they can be retained and stored for your onward use. In the background you are also stretching the connecting 'links' (actually these are tough energy bands) which bind the Spirit (Óðr) to the physical body (Lik). All this takes time. It is only when you have mastered all of these individual parts of the practice that you will be able to properly project.

Not a small task by any stretch of the imagination, but a critically essential one for your evolution. This is the key which opens up so many many locks...

# Failing to Fully Project with the Hugr

*Q: I've been doing the Huge Raven practice for ages now and still cannot fully project. How do I do it?*

The reason is simply that you are not meant to fully project by using this method. What the Huge Raven practice is doing is help you project awareness but not consciousness, or at least not fully. As you move your awareness and focus into the Raven it pulls only a small part of your consciousness. You may therefore notice that you are still fully aware of your physical body. This is to be expected.

In order to fully project you need to do the Spirit (Óðr) Projection. It is not until that late stage that you will have built up the flexibility of awareness AND consciousness needed to start with full projection out of the physical and energy body (Hamr).

Everything you will find in the books is intended to help you to build up various skills and abilities gradually until you get to the very end where you have developed them all to the point where projection is possible. Even then you will need to practice the outlined methods that may be shared along the way and then over a significant course of time to fully acquire the skill for the Spirit (Óðr) to perceive and function without the help of the energetic parts of the Self. It is literally like taking baby steps one after the other, unlocking each step in sequence until you can simply walk by your own devices, or put otherwise, be in your Spirit (Óðr) without needing supporting energetic structures. Then you take little steps one after the other in order to learn to function from within the Spirit (Óðr) without relying on the supporting systems. Having done all that you can start to train the Spirit (Óðr) to weed out imagination and wishful thinking from your perceptions AND finally after all of that you can go on with your exploring wherever it may lead you.

Unsurprisingly the entire process is very slow and gradual, and can take anywhere between six to twelve months of painfully slow and tedious daily practice until fully mastered. Needless to say it is worth each and every second spent attempting to master it.

# Loosing The Hugr or The Minni?

Q: *Can I lose my Hugr or Minni?*

This is one of the greatest fears of Oðin himself. The answer is yes, it is possible to lose your Hugr or Minni. There is always a danger to any form of evolution. The spiritual is no exception to the rule. It is a basic fundamental reality of life, no matter what level you are working on.

It is also true that you can minimise the risk of this occurring. This is done primarily by building as strong as possible a connection with those parts of the Self and by strengthening the connections built. For someone with a strongly integrated Self, if Ravens start to get lost, it becomes child's play to stretch out the Spirit (Óðr) or send forth the Fylgja to guide Ravens back 'home' to the host. The most powerful the Ravens are, the harder it is to divert them off their course. It is for this reason that in The Spirit of Húnir Awakens we spent a lot of time and effort to develop the ability to separate the Hugr and Minni gradually at a very slow pace. This practice serves to give the Ravens cohesion, which in turn enables them to store more power. Additionally, it helps the other parts of your Self to observe and familiarise itself with what is happening which in turn helps those parts which are able to keep track and supervise what is going on to do so.

Finally, when you learnt to unleash the runic energies from within those parts of your Self, the whole Self familiarises itself with those very currents. This in turn gives the Self the ability to connect with the runic energies without needing for conscious direction to direct it. In times of crisis, a highly developed Hugr and Minni can directly make use of those currents in order to get out of 'crisis situations'. This should all serve to explain the flow and progression of your learning and why emphasis was placed on shaping things slowly and organically (at least at the level of the Self).

# HEALING THE MIND
&
IMPROVING LIFE

# Dealing with Obsessions and Addictions

*Q: How do I Help Someone with an Obsession or an Addiction?*

Before looking into this, a few words of caution. First and foremost, you cannot do all the heavy lifting for someone else. Ultimately only that person can deal with it. Second, due to the nature of obsessions and addictions, they can be very dangerous on a mental level. The thought-streams are typically so powerful that they can easily pull the person trying to help into the obsession or addiction. This is one of the reasons why, as part of their vocational training, professional psychologists have to undergo constant counselling themselves. Battles against obsessions and addictions are best left to the professionals. However, in the interest of tackling the subject matter, we will look at what is actually happening on the mental level of reality which practitioners might not be aware of.

In *The Spirit of Húnir Awakens*[1, 5], we talked about the fundamental principle of 'like attracts like' on the mental level of reality. Understanding this is essential. When dealing with obsessions and addictions, and looking at addressing these conditions, the principle of 'like attracts like' is at play but in a deeply negative manner. With all thoughts we express, process, work with and so forth, the same principles apply indiscriminately such that such thoughts are amplified manifold. Obsessions are born out of an interest which gradually becomes stronger and stronger. The underlying thoughts which give rise to obsessive compulsions pull in more and more thoughts which are like them. In other words, more and more thoughts about that very interest gather up and overwhelm.

Eventually, a person consumed by its thoughts adds so much mental energy to these thoughts (which collectively are a thought-stream), that in addition to simply pulling in more thoughts that are alike, energy which is alike also attracted or pulled in. This results in a dual stream of thoughts pulling in more thought and the energy (or mental gravity) as a more forceful and more pronounced current, which then in its own right attracts or pulls in more energies which are like those expressed by the initial thought-stream. This in turn empowers the thought-stream, which then increases its gravitational pull. At this point, we have energy, gravity and thought and the trinity is formed. The thought-stream via the energy gathered will therefore gain shape and the shape will always match the initial interest symbolically.

This in turn suddenly makes it not only perceptible by the Spirit (Óðr) and Mind (Hugr) but also allows it to reach into the energy body's (Hamr) perceptual mechanisms (which perceive energies rather than thoughts). This elevated level of perception will excite the energetic body (Hamr) into a more lucid state (noted that the energetic body (Hamr) is usually in stasis whilst we live in the physical). In turn, this leads to the energetic body (Hamr) 'liking' that energy more and more, and wanting more of it. It is exactly the same principle which gives rise to addictions. Those who smoke their first cigarette have an unpleasant experience, then the second is nicer, the third even more so and so forth, until smoking becomes a desire that feeds into a need for that desire to be met. Unless the energy body (Hamr) is aware enough to reject the energy or the will strong enough to break out of the thought-stream, this now dangerous combination takes over and demands "feeding". As a state built by the Self, it is not perceived as an external threat or foreign influence, and is welcomed by the Self. It is entirely a Self creation and hence part of that Self. Even more so, since the energy body (Hamr) is directly connected to the physical body (Lik), its enjoyment of these energies will trigger physiological responses in the body itself, typically to record contentment or satisfaction when the obsession or addition is nourished.

The danger is when the obsession or addiction becomes grounded in the flesh. At this point, the energy body (Hamr) keeps on triggering physiological responses and the physical body's nervous and chemical systems kick into action in direct response to the energy body's stimulus. At this point, the initial interest now has a mental, energetic and physiological footing. The brain conditions itself, the nervous system anchors it, and the entire bio-chemical dimension of the physical body (Lik) adapts to it. Effectively, the obsession or addiction becomes one with the Self and its extraction all the harder requiring a re-wiring of the Self in its entirety by applying physiological, energetic and mental tools to prune the obsessions and addictions out.

It is not enough just to deal with the energetic side of things. The physical biology will just pull in more of that energy type, as will the newly formed mental thought-stream. Even if the mental AND energetic side are dealt with, the physical biology will crave its influences and eventually rebuild it all from ground up using the Shadow Self (Sal).

For this reason, being in control of one's thoughts, having the ability to directly use the mental parts of the Self and developing a good grasp of silencing the mind is absolutely essential. All these tools are invaluable to short cut the formation process of negative thought-streams before they ever gain the ability to start pulling in energy or gaining any type of mental gravity of their own by default.

If you really want to help someone suffering from these conditions, teach them how to silence their mind. Each time a thought in any way related to their obsession or addiction come forward, let them silence the mind to stop those thoughts from gaining strength and momentum. Energetically, you will have to either purge all that energy from their system (which will result in an energy craving) or transform it into some other type of energy via the alchemy of the < Kaun (Kenaz) rune. This will not do away with the need to get mediation advice and treatment to deal with the physiological side of things. It would be unsound for any beginner to use runic influences to interfere with a nervous system to avoid medical treatment. Doing so without perfect senses on all levels of reality can cause far more damage and harm.

# Using 'Like Attracts Like' to Improve Life

*Q: How Do I Use the Like-Attracts-Like Principle to Influence my Own Life for the Better?*

An excellent question. We have discussed this to great extent in *The Spirit of Húnir Awakens* but it might be worth putting it in context by using a few examples.

The general rule is that what you think is what you attract, and pull into your life, you harmonise with.

This can lead to many interests, wanted (as well as unwanted) effects. For instance, when you find that you are constantly attracting the wrong type of person or persons into your life, this principle is at play. In fact, it is the cause of the type of individuals that enter into your life. It is also at play (along with fate itself) when you suddenly meet someone who is a perfect match (be it as a friend, lover or colleague). A person will respond to the energies around you, to their vibrational influences and to what thoughts surround you. These frequencies and vibrations establish a pattern which in turn draws them in, providing of course that their own interest (thoughts), energies and so forth match yours to a certain extent. The more they match, the stronger the pull will be experienced. When fate plays a hand in the process, things are a little different. In such cases, these matching patterns are established whilst in the presence of that person by what people often term the 'hand of fate' (there is no such hand but its influence is there). We will look at the interplay of fate in greater detail in further works. Suffice to say that these types of encounters are always aimed at providing one or the other or even both individuals an opportunity for evolutionary and spiritual growth (otherwise it would not be fated to happen). As such, in most cases dealing with uncomfortable or even downright difficult situations is required in order to move forward. Such events are of great value both by providing the opportunity to only resolve inner issues which act as blocks (blocks we more often than not get stuck in) but also by providing us with invaluable opportunities of accelerated growth. These opportunities will typically arise from the fact that the people who trigger them will (more often than not) be of a higher spiritual maturity and come into your live to boost your own progress or maturation.

    Taken in another context, you can easily (or, in other words, with little discipline), not only add new elements into your life such as desired experiences, but also remove unwanted ones. It all boils down to gaining control of your own thoughts. Let us say for instance that you are seeking more financial stability in your life. Most people do. By focussing on a regular basis on what you think will bring you such stability, and mastering fuelling those thoughts with runic energy or life force, you will attract that stability in a far more pronounced way into your life. Once these attributes or characteristics start to manifest, you mentally welcome it into your life and its potency will accelerate.

    You can use the same practice to throw out those influences you do not want in your life. Simply pay attention to the thoughts which give rise to them. Usually these would be negatives. For instance, most people focus on the lack of money when seeking wealth thus bringing in more 'lack of wealth' instead. Each time you catch yourself thinking how you lack wealth, do not have enough money, need more money and so forth, simply interrupt the flow of thought and think of its direct opposite. At first this will prove very challenging but eventually those negatives will loose energy or grip, each time interrupted they will be deprived a little more energy. Then by immediately countering that with its directly opposite positive, it will cause the two to start cancelling each other other. Your goal will be reached once you have not only cancelled out all the negatives but also swung the balance in the opposite direction. As usual PERSISTANCE and PERSEVERANCE are the two great keys!

# DEEP THEORY

# Energy, Runes, 'Magic' Are They Real?

*Q: Do Energies, Runes, 'Magic' and the so-called Supernatural Actually Exist or Not?*

A fascinating question I come across on a VERY regular basis, in addition to being asked 'Why does this or that not work for me?' Most would simply argue 'Of course it exists' or 'Of course it does not', depending on their personal views, beliefs and experiences. To some people, unless it has been 'proven' by science in a finding or other (no matter how intrinsically flawed that science may be), or if an event has not been reported by a 'reliable' source, it simply never happened, is not true or is a lie. For others who live within the energetic reality on a daily basis, the answer would be an automatic: 'Of course it does'. So which is right?

Well, this might come as a shock to many, but they both are. Perplexing, is it not? How can opposites at such an extreme level of the scale, of an absolute no and an absolute yes, both be correct?

The answer stands – both views are correct. The reason for this is actually very simple. For those of you who have read *The Spirit of Húnir Awakens*[1,5] it might seem obvious, and for those who have not had the opportunity, I would recommend you pick up a copy right now!

In *The Spirit of Húnir Awakens* we have seen how thought gathers energetic gravity, then form and finally the time dimensionality in order to manifest. The energetic gravity gives all thoughts a form (or space) dimensionality which then, if conditions are right, spills from the subtler energetic level (what people typically call the astral) into the denser ones (which are typically termed the physical). At this point they gain dimensionality of time and are able to manifest in our daily perceptions. We have looked at how Spirit was created by Húnir in *The Spirit of Húnir Awakens (Part 1)*[1], and the same universal principles apply to EVERYTHING.

Back to our question: 'How can both these opposing views be correct?' Thoughts gather on the mental, which is unformed and not subject to time or space. In addition to this, the principle of 'Like attracts Like' is in operation at its strongest there (due to absence of space or time to slow this attraction down). For an individual who is all about science and proving this or that, what they will be experiencing is a reality where ONLY those things – experiences and so forth – conforming to their beliefs exist. Anything which contradicts them will simply not be perceived by that individuals' mind. On the contrary, those who have the belief that energy exists and plays a direct role will have a broader perceptual mechanism in play and will perceive all those parts of reality. To such an individual, the answer is: 'Of course it exists!' Because they see and experience it. It is all a matter of belief leading to certain thought patterns which attract like. These thought patterns gain gravity and eventually manifest in reality.

This is what is typically hinted at when people talk about vibrating on a higher level. It is nothing to do with actual vibrational level, but rather it has to do with how our minds function. We are here looking at the cause (the mental perceptual capabilities) not the effect (the vibrational increase). The mind starts to perceive at a 'higher' level of reality, which in turn increases the scope of the individual who is perceiving, hence the actuality of vibrational increase.

'But wait!' I hear you say. 'The physical things happen due to energy manipulation irrespective of what someone might believe or not. How does that work?'

True, the physical (or more accurately, the denser energetic level of manifestation) does manifest things which originate beyond the scope of belief, thought or mental capabilities of a person. It is because here (in Midgard), everything manifests. What will typically happen is the strongest of two or more conflicting events (the one with the most energetic gravity) will manifest. If someone who mentally rejects the possibility of experiencing such an event / occurrence, one of two things will happen:

> First: they could try to explain it in a manner which is compatible with their perceptual limitations. Ever come across a hard sceptic who will try to explain anything away? Even if it does not quite make perfect logical sense?

> Second: Disbelief kicks in. The mind goes into a type of shock – or rather paralysis – for a very brief time (it can be a second or two, or more, depending on

the individual), then convinces itself that the event never actually occurred in the first place. A discomfort is experienced, which as more and more time passes is replaced by a conviction that whatever caused it had never happened.

In some rare cases, the individual will actually question what they witnessed, and that will open up the possibility into expansion of mental perceptual capabilities through the search for answers. In most, however, either scenario 1 or 2 listed above will take hold, and that will be the end of the matter.

For the energetically aware, it will be a matter of normality. Yes, that person might still investigate what occurred and why, but its possibility of occurrence will be a given. If the event is not physically manifest but remains a purely energetic one, the mind which rejects those levels of reality will fail to conform to the 'like attracts like' laws and simply fail to perceive the event.

It is the mental bubbles we isolate ourselves in which restrict or open up our perceptual capabilities. This is one of the reasons why we are, on a daily basis, being told how things work and why they work, in this or that way. Those thoughts, repeated often enough without conscious rejection, condition us into limiting our awareness and hence our perceptual capabilities. Such limitation then convinces us that the broader spectrum of reality simply does not exist and we loose our ability to perceive it. This in turn limits us completely. So do energy and magic and runes exist? They do, but only for those who can perceive them. For everyone else they go unperceived. Nevertheless, these people will have to experience their effects, irrespective of their rejections.

Want to increase your energetic capabilities? When practicing being in the Spirit (Óðr) on a daily basis, add the meditation that your Óðr is walking through the mental reality of our world where energy, runes and magic exist. Your energy bodies (Hamr) will respond in kind because you will be attracting all things that are LIKE your thoughts, and will become capable of perceiving – as well as channelling – a broader spectrum of reality. It takes time – persistence is the key! The stronger you establish that belief, the more energetic gravity will be built and the faster you will manifest this shift in perception whilst being physically grounded. It is a matter of pushing out the old, limiting mindset and replacing it with something which you want instead. Simple, effective and easy, is it not?

    And now you know why both views are correct, each in its own way.

# Spirit Vibrational Rates & Time

*Q: Insight into Spirit Vibrational Rates and Time*

Time is, spiritually speaking, a result of energetic gravity. Yes, we are talking about the same gravitational forces as understood by the scientific communities here. Condensation of the energetic, under the direction of the impulses generated by the principle of 'like attracts like', on the mental level of reality, gives rise to energetic gravity. This gravity then intensifies and condenses even further, giving rise to what we can loosely term physical manifestation – in other words, the universe we are all so familiar with.

Once you have gravity, you have resistance and various kinetic forces / energies come into play. Their interaction (governed by the runes ᚱ Reið (Raidho), ᚾ Nauð (Nauthiz) and ᚲ Kaun (Kenaz)) establish time. Energetically speaking, time is a quantitative force which can be measured by the amount of substance (or force) and energy manifest at any given point. This substance will fade as a natural result of it exercising influence in creation. How fast it fades, how much of it has been used and so forth, establishes the effects of time upon creation. Just as we have the unalterable principle of 'like attracts like' on the mental / spiritual level of reality, we also have time as an overriding principle on the physical (or, if you prefer, the condensed energetic) side of reality.

Why all this discussion regarding time? It is only by gaining a little insight into it that we can understand how it impacts us in terms of energy and spiritual experiences. We will look at this in a lot of detail at a later point in time, but for now it is worth considering its impact on the spirit.

Each Spirit (Óðr) vibrates at a certain rate and frequency. This is determined by its maturity, its inheritance (yes, our spirits also inherit; more on this later on), its underlying characteristics and available substances. As we have just seen, time is an energetic phenomenon and hence it too has a vibrational rate. When your spirit's vibrational rate increases its interaction with time, then time's influence also changes. Hence we see that the vibrational flow and increases in strength of a Spirit (Óðr) speed up its experiences of time. This is when you experience the phenomenon of living through many experiences in a seemingly short amount of time. When adding spirit, mental projection and direct mental perceptions to this mix (which are timeless), the resulting accumulation of direct experiential growth can be downright phenomenal. Those of us experiencing this type of living can gain life experiences so rapidly that a sense of rapid aging (or rather maturing) occurs, due to our perceptions of time and life. This is why connecting to the so called 'inner child' (which is a manifestation of your biological awareness, and we will look at this in a lot of detail in *The Blood of Lóðurr Awakens*[3]) is so important, it serves the purpose of constantly regenerating the Self and refreshing the perceptions of the self by the Self. This process of accelerated experiencing (where one gains hundreds if not thousands of years' worth of experiences that a human being would normally perceive in a space of hours, days or weeks) is what results in hyper-evolution.

# Why Do Spirits Seek Love?

*Q: Why do Spirits Seek Love?*

The simple answer is they do not. It is a common misunderstanding that what mankind defines as 'love' is a universal thing which every consciousness seeks out – a misunderstanding which is overly promoted, at that. Love is our biological awareness reaching out towards someone, for one reason or another. This is also why what we call love has a chemical reaction in the brain and an entire series of responses in our physiologies. Is it not real, then? Quite the contrary. Remember our biology also has consciousness and it too needs to evolve and grow. Not only that but our Spirit (Óðr) experiences through it and with it.

What it causes is a rapid (sometimes instant) harmonisation of two beings on a biological level, which then rapidly tunes the energetic similarities those two possess. By amplifying those similarities with the resulting energy created when we fall in love, they develop into 'sameness'. This in turn brings them together even more.

Conflict can and often does arise due to one problem: the biological awareness not only triggers but imposes love upon the mind. It decides and sets up triggers throughout our whole biology to follow. Hence you get the constant thinking about the person you are in love with, the increase in heartbeat, the excitement when seeing them, the impulse to reach out and so forth. This also gives us insight into so-called socially 'forbidden' forms of love. Social norms are established by the minds of humans. Love is dictated by our biology, which completely ignores the mind. This can also sometimes result in confusion because the two (mind and body) might not be (and usually are not) in synchronous agreement. It is also why so-called 'straight' individuals can suddenly find themselves attracted to the same gender and gay individuals to the opposite gender. All these phenomena are direct manifestations of biological choice. Yes, we consciously pursue our love interests or not, but the triggers are purely biological.

For our Spirit (Óðr), experiencing this is a boon. The overriding influence of the physiology forces it to seek out harmonisation, not only with our biology but also with the one we fall in love with. What is important is the falling in love, but not all love needs to be reciprocated, and at times it is not intended to be. In these situations, the two individuals involved will become good friends. The important thing for the spirit is that it has fallen in love, that very experience is what is required. It happens in order to stop the higher evolved spirits becoming arrogant in their Self. All too often, evolution results in arrogance of Being, and seeing one's peers as lesser to the self. Tools such as love are used to remind the spirit of the importance of those it would misperceive as lesser. When love is reciprocated (truly, rather than just saying 'I love you too' when that is not the case), it is not always just for the benefit of the evolving individual Spirit (Óðr), but can also be for the one who is highly evolved as well. Matured spirits often have immense problems and struggles when it comes to dealing with physicality. It is not their strong point; left to their own devices, they tend to avoid it as much as possible rather than learn from it or their struggles, in dealing with their own physicality, which gives rise to resentment and a sense of loss. Being in love with a spirit which is still maturing (those spirits are often extremely adept at dealing with physicality) provides them with the assistance they require to master physicality. Such relationships can literally turn out to be one partner providing the foundation upon which the other can rely. In reverse, the partner seeking evolution finds an incredible teacher and enabler in their other half. One of them gains assistance with physicality and the other gains hyper-evolution, which those not in such a relationship cannot even dream of.

This in turn can lead (depending on the individuals) to greater spiritual growth, a widening of possibilities, a complimenting of characteristics and so forth. This is where we enter the domain of spirit creation and evolution with another. A most fascinating and intricate one...

# Masculine vs Feminine
## Biological Polarities

*Q: Why Bother With the Masculine Vs. Feminine Polarities?*

Quite simply, we are not the same. Each one of us is totally unique and hence individual. The modern social misperception of everyone being equal and hence the same is nothing more than an illusion, or at worst, a denial of individuality in an attempt to force a collective mindset on the masses.

We are unique and strive towards further 'uniqueness'. Masculine and feminine polarities are there to give expression at both the natural and universal levels to further uniqueness. Men and women have specific biological reasons as to what makes them male and female. We have different gender-specific DNA, brain formations, bio-chemistry and energetic polarities, including key differences in our Hvels (the Norse equivalent of the chakras or energy centres in various parts of the Self). That is simple, cold hard fact.

Much work is being done to reinterpret things to include all sorts of deviations from these two polarities, in an attempt to introduce a third androgynous one. However, all that is actually taking place is the production of a lesser expression of one's own original biological maleness or femaleness. Looking at it from the energetic angle, what is being achieved is a stifling of expression of the masculine or feminine currents. Mankind has a mix of the two in both genders, but everyone is essentially dominant in one or the other, with the opposite polarity just adding 'flavour' to the original. In the Old Norse culture, for instance, when a man allowed too great a feminine influence in his nature to emerge, he was labelled as 'ergi' and subject to great social shame. It was a direct criticism on a social level of his loss of masculinity, a loss of his nature. Why was there no such shame for women? Simply because of the understanding of energetic realities and how they worked. The masculine current (or polarity, if you prefer) evolved out of the feminine, hence for a man who is an expression the masculine to shift back into the feminine to such a point that its energy took over was seen as shameful and would be shunned. For a woman evolving along the feminine, there was no such shame, as there was no energetic backtracking in evolutionary terms. It is all a very complex energetic set of interactions. Essentially, thinking of it as the masculine branching out of the feminine current, and evolving in parallel to the original feminine current, is the clearest way of conceptualising this. Once separated, there is no return back, other than in terms of reversing evolution to the point of the original separation.

For the Gods, this was a simple matter, due to their mastery of both polarities. Shapeshifting from male to female was not only practiced, but was done in such a manner that total femininity was fully embodied in their new forms, to the point where Loki was able to give birth as would any woman. He became a complete, perfect woman. But do keep in mind that all these shapeshifts, even those of Oðin, were only temporary, and they would always return to their original male forms. Interestingly, Goddesses shifting into male counterparts is seldom if ever mentioned. Many will argue that this is due to a male bias of the storytellers, but those who understand how energy works will know that it is actually due to the energetic evolutionary patterns instead. It is easy to go backwards or forwards, but it is insanely difficult to branch out of an evolutionary stream into a totally unknown spin-off without some external influencer imbuing consciousness with a full range of experiences of that new branch of evolution.

Back to the human perspective: it blinds us to our uniqueness when thinking that we are all the 'same', regardless of gender. Our bodies are the foundation of growth of consciousness and expansion of Spirit (Óðr), and ignoring or rejecting our own physiology would be far too damaging to our growth. Instead, we take it into account when working on our evolution and by showing respect to it and to each other, we move towards even greater individualisation, and hence a greater range of expression of our own masculinity or femininity (depending on which of these polarities we were born to express). We take ourselves as we are, not as we would like to be. Reality vs. illusionary, actuality vs. desire – that is the struggle. Yes, we will each express our own masculinity / femininity in our own unique individual way, but that is exactly what we should be doing. The social stereotypes are there because they are expressions of what these polarities have evolved to be in human terms, and they will evolve again without the need for us to deny or twist them. Respect your Self, whatever shape it takes. The biological awareness you have is essential to your very being.

# Rune Mystics And Religious Practices

*Q: Religion – Should Rune Mystics Follow or Avoid Certain Religious Practices?*

Religion seems to be a very popular topic. I have briefly touched upon it in the previous *The Breath of Oðin Awakens – Questions & Answers* but it is worth looking at once more in view of the additional new insights developed within *The Spirit of Húnir Awakens*.

Before delving into the topic, it is important to keep context in mind. What this is referring to is the fact that a spiritually maturing rune mystic takes the cosmic – or if you prefer, universal – view of things and not the socio-human one. Maturation of spirit has gradually moved the individual from the socio-human to the cosmic / universal (or as it is often referred to: 'The Big Picture'). The way their mind looks at things undergoes radical shifts and significant changes which, more often than not, appear totally incomprehensible to their peers. Hence these words will be totally obvious to those maturing, yet at the same time very harsh to the understanding of those who are yet struggling to do so.

    From the rune mystic's point of view, namely the universal, there is no need for religion at all. They have worked through and passed beyond the need for any form of religion whatsoever. There is no need for the rigid guidance of religious doctrine and discipline. They are at a point where those teachings would simply impose too many limitations upon them. Their maturation imbues them with freedom and fluidity as well as independence of spirit. They no longer need to bow to any deity in order to gain its favour (or attention, for that matter) in exchange for guidance and assistance in spiritual growth.

    The mystic might not know yet exactly where they are heading, but they most certainly do know that when they are on the right track, their intuitive knowing will be all that is needed to guide them. They see the all-too-popular concepts of 'heaven' and 'hell' as nothing more than perceptions of states of being and energy, and they are able to, by an act of pure will, shift into whatever reality or world they desire or need to be in. They no longer need to work with a specific being or divinity, for they can identify with their essences.

    Can the mystic still interact and learn from them? Naturally: learning never stops; the journey keeps on going. The important thing to keep in mind is that the mystic will learn from such a being, be it a god, a spirit, a giant, or whatever else, and when there is no longer a need to do so, they will move away from this in their struggle forward. They never bind themselves to any single being or group of beings, be they positive or negative, gods or ghosts; that would be a burden and limitation too costly for the evolution of their spirit. Instead, due to their fluidity and flexibility, they can learn from them and move on when the time is right, never sacrificing their independence and freedoms, never binding themselves to one single entity. Thus, the scope of their mind will keep on expanding with new possibilities, and their spirit will grow through a constant increase of experiences, never restricted or bound to any one place or entity. They are fluid, changing and persisting as life, ever seeking new experiences and new forms of expression of their own Self, ever expanding and ever evolving.

    To answer the question in view of these insights is simple. They see all religions as unnecessary limitations for their own Self, but as necessary evolutionary crutches for those still learning to walk within the various levels of reality. They will understand and know of the inner principles or essence of all religious manifestations, but never follow their dogmas or limit themselves to these teachings, because a true mystic can walk through creation on his or her own merit. At the pinnacle of maturation, they eventually embody Divinity in every aspect of their own Self, and all existence willingly serves them, rather than the other way around.

# APPENDIX

## References & Footnotes

1. Frank A. Rúnaldrar (2017). The Spirit of Hunir Awakens (Part 1) - Norse Keys to the Spirit, Mind & Perception, 41. London: Bastian & West. ISBN: 978-0-9955343-2-2

2. ante. p.13

3. Frank A. Rúnaldrar (2018). The Blood of Lóðurr Awakens. London: Bastian & West. ISBN: 978-0-9955343-6-0

4. Frank A. Rúnaldrar (2017) The Breath of Oðin Awakens - Secrets of the Norse Hamingja & Luck-Fuelled Breath. 2nd Edition. London: Bastian & West. ISBN: 978-0-9955343-4-6

5. Frank A. Rúnaldrar (2017) The Spirit of Hunir Awakens (Part 2) - The Norse 'Holy Grail'. London: Bastian & West. ISBN: 978-0-9955343-3-9

7. ante (1), p.70

8. ante (5), p. 131

www.ingramcontent.com/pod-product-compliance
Lightning Source LLC
Chambersburg PA
CBHW031413040426
42444CB00005B/553